Watch and Pray

JoAnn Davis

Illustrations by: Dwight Nacaytuna

To order additional copies of this book, contact:
Xlibris
1-888-795-4274
www.Xlibris.com
Orders@Xlibris.com

(A Book for Children)
Ages 3-8

Written by
JoAnn Davis

Watch Your Feet

Prayer

Lord, help me not to kick people or animals in Jesus name!

Watch Your Hands

Prayer

Lord, help me not to steal or take anything that does not belong to me in Jesus name!

Watch Your Face and Eyes

Prayer

Lord, help me not to make funny faces or roll my eyes at my parents or other people in Jesus name!

Prayer

Lord, help me not to say bad or
curse words in Jesus name!

Watch Your Anger

Prayer

Lord, help me not to get angry when I can't have my way or do what I want in Jesus name!

Watch Your Selfishness

Prayer

Lord, teach me not to be selfish and help me to share with others in Jesus name!

Watch Your Manners

Prayer

Lord, help me to say please when I ask
for something or say thank you when
I receive something in Jesus name!

Prayer

Lord, help me to think good
thoughts in Jesus name!

Watch Your Heart

Prayer

Lord, help me to have a heart to help others in Jesus name!